The Baroque Trombone

12 Repertoire pieces from the Golden Age for trombone and keyboard

Le Trombone baroque

12 pièces de répertoire pour trombone et piano
empruntées à l'âge d'or de la musique

Die Posaune im Barock

12 Repertoirestücke aus der Blütezeit des Barock
für Posaune und Klavier

Selected and arranged by Simon Wills

© 1997 by Faber Music Ltd
First Published in 1997 by Faber Music Ltd
3 Queen Square London WC1N 3AU
Cover design by S & M Tucker
Cover illustration © Haags Gemeente Museum Amstelveen, Holland
Music engraved by Wessex Music Services
Printed in England by Halstan & Co Ltd

ISBN 0 571 51723 4

ff
FABER
MUSIC

Foreword

This book is designed to be a lively introduction to baroque music. Two pieces, the Biber and the Cesare, were originally written for the trombone and in its original form the Handel gives much of the melody to the first trombone. The others are transcriptions. Pieces were chosen to explore a wide range of styles from this period without making life difficult for a young player: the music has been freely transposed to avoid awkward slide shifts and unreasonably high notes, and the ornaments have been written out. Where it has been possible to ornament the music in accordance with authentic practice, I have done so but where there was a conflict between historical correctness and ease of playing, the latter has always won. You may be surprised that the Bach family is represented only by the relatively obscure W.F. Bach, but J.S. Bach in particular may be found in several other publications and the curious style of W.F. Bach's Polonaises is particularly well suited to the trombone.

The essence of good baroque performance is to play with great freedom and expressiveness: small details are important. For this reason, by all means take the metronome markings as a guide to speed but avoid playing the pieces rigidly in tempo.

Simon Wills 1997

Vorwort

Die vorliegende Sammlung ist als lebendige Einführung in die Musik des Barock gedacht. Zwei der ausgewählten Stücke, die Werke von Biber und Cesare, wurden im Original für Posaune geschrieben, und in der Originalfassung des bei uns wiedergegebenen Satzes aus Händels *Saul* ist die erste Posaune in starkem Umfang Melodieträger. Die anderen Stücke sind sämtlich Bearbeitungen für Posaune. Die Werke wurden mit dem Ziel ausgesucht, möglichst große stilistische Vielfalt ohne übermässige Schwierigkeiten für den jungen Spieler zu bieten. Häufig wurden die Stücke transponiert, um ungeschickte Tonverbindungen und besonders exponierte hohe Töne zu vermeiden, die Verzierungen wurden ausgeschrieben. Wo immer möglich, wurden Verzierungsanweisungen gegeben, die den Prinzipien damaliger Aufführungspraxis entsprechen. In Fällen, wo sich zwischen historischer Authentizität und der Spielbarkeit Konflikte ergaben, wurde jedoch immer zugunsten der leichteren Ausführung entschieden. Überraschend ist vielleicht, daß die Musikerfamilie Bach nur durch den relativ wenig bekannten Wilhelm Friedemann vertreten ist; Werke von Johann Sebastian Bach findet man aber in mehreren anderen Publikationen und der ausgefallen Stil von Wilhelm Friedemann Bachs Polonaisen eignet sich besonders gut zur Interpretation auf der Posaune.

Historisch korrekt musizierte Barockmusik ist geprägt durch große künstlerische Freiheit und starken Ausdruck, kleinen Details kommt große Bedeutung zu. Deshalb sollte man die Metronomangaben als Vorschlag ansehen und die Stücke keinesfalls nur präzis durchzählen.

Simon Wills 1997

Simon Wills was born in 1957. He began his career in the opera house at Palermo and then spent some years in the London Symphony Orchestra. He is now principal trombone of the Chamber Orchestra of Europe and plays first trombone in the Freiburg Baroque Orchestra and many other ensembles. He is a professor of trombone and historic brass style at the Guildhall School of Music and Drama in London.

Simon Wills ist Jarhgang 1957. Er begann seine Karriere mit einem Engagement am Opernhaus in Palermo und war dann einige Jahre Mitglied des London Symphony Orchestra. Er ist jetzt Erster Posaunist beim Chamber Orchestra of Europe, und spielt im Freiburger Barockorchester und in vielen anderen Ensembles. Gleichzeitig ist er Professor für Posaune und historische Musik Für Blechbläser an der Guildhall School of Music and Drama in London.

Che faro
(from *Orfeo ed Euridice*)

C. W. von Gluck
(1714 - 1787)

Andante (♩ = 120)

Polonaise No. 6

W. F. Bach
(1710 - 1784)

Adagio, molto liberamente ($\quad$ = 48)

La Hieronyma

G. M. Cesare
(c. 1590 - 1667)

Largo
(from *Cello Concerto in E♭*)

A. Vivaldi
(1678 - 1741)

Pavan de Spaigne

M. Praetorius
(1571 - 1621)

The Baroque Trombone

12 Repertoire pieces from the Golden Age for trombone and keyboard

Le Trombone baroque

12 pièces de répertoire pour trombone et piano
empruntées à l'âge d'or de la musique

Die Posaune im Barock

12 Repertoirestücke aus der Blütezeit des Barock
für Posaune und Klavier

Selected and arranged by Simon Wills

© 1997 by Faber Music Ltd
First Published in 1997 by Faber Music Ltd
3 Queen Square London WC1N 3AU
Cover design by S & M Tucker
Cover illustration © Haags Gemeente Museum Amstelveen, Holland
Music engraved by Wessex Music Services
Printed in England by Halstan & Co Ltd
All rights reserved

ISBN 0 571 51723 4

FABER MUSIC

3

Che faro
(from *Orfeo ed Euridice*)

4C. W. von Gluck
(1714 - 1787)

5© 1997 by Faber Music Ltd.

6This music is copyright. Photocopying is illegal.

Polonaise No. 6

W. F. Bach
(1710 - 1784)

Adagio, molto liberamente (♩ = 48)

La Hieronyma

G. M. Cesare
(c. 1590 - 1667)

7

Largo
(from *Cello Concerto in E♭*)

A. Vivaldi
(1678 - 1741)

Pavan de Spaigne

M. Praetorius
(1571 - 1621)

0

0

0

When I am Laid in Earth

(from *Dido and Aeneas*)

H. Purcell
(1659 - 1695)

Forlane
(from *Les Sybarites*)

J. P. Rameau
(1683 - 1764)

* Play the upper note if seventh position is out of reach.

Die obere Note spielen, wenn die siebte Position nicht erreichbar ist.

© 1997 by Faber Music Ltd.

Allemande
(from the *4th Concert Royal*)

F. Couperin
(1668 - 1733)

Adagio and Allegro

H. Biber
(1644 - 1704)

Volta

M. Praetorius
(1571 - 1621)

Dead March
(from *Saul*)

G. F. Handel
(1685 - 1759)

Hypochondria (1st Movement)
(from *Six Concerti Written in a Hurry - 1723*)

Jan Dismas Zelenka
(1679 - 1755)

When I am Laid in Earth

(from *Dido and Aeneas*)

H. Purcell
(1659 - 1695)

Largo (♩ = 60)

Forlane
(from *Les Sybarites*)

J. P. Rameau
(1683 - 1764)

Lively (♩. = 84)

* Play the upper note if seventh position is out of reach.
  Die obere Note spielen, wenn die siebte Position nicht erreichbar ist.

Allemande
(from the *4th Concert Royal*)

F. Couperin
(1668 - 1733)

Flowing (♩ = 72)

Adagio and Allegro

H. Biber
(1644 - 1704)

Volta

M. Praetorius
(1571 - 1621)

Dead March
(from *Saul*)

G. F. Handel
(1685 - 1759)

Hypochondria (1st Movement)

(from *Six Concerti Written in a Hurry - 1723*)

Jan Dismas Zelenka
(1679 - 1755)

Sprightly, but not fast (♩ = 72)

Notes

Che Faro Senza Euridice?
From *Orfeo ed Euridice*
CHRISTOPH WILLIBALD VON GLUCK (1714-1787)

The title means "what shall I do without Eurydice?" It is sung by Orfeo when, having led his dead wife out of Hades, he defies the Gods by turning to look at her and loses her for a second time. His lamentations are interrupted by the god Amore, who restores Eurydice to him amid general rejoicing. It is a sad song, but don't play it too slowly.

Polonaise No.6
WILHELM FRIEDEMANN BACH (1710-1784)

This introspective piece is a good example of the 'Empfindsamkeit' (sensitive) style favoured by Wilhelm Bach and his brother Carl Philip Emmanuel. Play about with the tempo a lot, and make a meal of every phrase! The original key, E♭ minor, makes the music sound decidely unearthly if, as it used to be in Bach's day, it is played on an unequally tempered keyboard.

La Hieronyma
GIOVANNI MARTINO CESARE (c.1590-1667)

Cesare was a cornetto player who worked in Bavaria. This solo is taken from a collection that he published in 1621. Conventions in performance were so well known in his day that the composer gave few indications. I have therefore added a great many dynamics and phrasing indications, as well as points of imitation in the piano part. The piece should to some extent sound like an improvisation.

Largo from Cello Concerto in E♭
ANTONIO VIVALDI (1678-1741)

Vivaldi, who was known as the "Red Priest" because of the startling colour of his hair, worked at an orphanage and music school in Venice. The solo part should be played in a singing style - quavers are quite long notes at this speed. When the intervals become wide, as they do in a couple of places, it is better to slacken the tempo a little rather than let the notes become stifled or snatched.

Two dances Volta and Pavan de Spaigne
MICHAEL PRAETORIUS (1571-1621)

The Volta was a vigorous dance for couples: on each dotted note the gentleman would hurl his partner into the air on his knee revealing her petticoats and ankles to public view. A little vulgarity of expression would not go amiss here. The *Pavan de Spaigne* was a more stately affair, and this one will repay a very lyrical approach.

When I am Laid in Earth
From *Dido and Aeneas*
HENRY PURCELL (1659-1695)

Dido and Aeneas was written in 1689 ". . . to be performed at Mr Josiah Priest's Boarding School at Chelsea by young Gentlewomen". In the last part Dido, rejected by her lover

Aeneas, sings this famous aria as she dies. The repeated notes in the second half are given the words "Remember me, but ah! forget my fate". On the trombone the piece works best if played with some momentum but with a very intense tone quality.

Forlane from Les Sybarites
JEAN PHILIPPE RAMEAU (1683-1764)

Rameau was an organist and theoretician whose extraordinary success as an opera composer did not come until he was past fifty. This is a straightforward country dance which should be played vigorously with a strong beat.

Allemande from the 4th Concert Royal
FRANÇOIS COUPERIN (1668-1733)

The *Concerts Royeaux* were written at Versailles to entertain Louis X1V on Sundays during 1714 and 1715. Their instrumentation was not fixed; violin, oboe and flute were used for the solo parts on different occasions. The music was lavishly ornamented in performance: the ornaments given here lie easily on the slide and will be no trouble if played steadily and with a good sense of line.

Adagio and Allegro
From *Sonata for 2 violins, trombone and continuo*
HEINRICH BIBER (1644-1704)

In the seventeenth century the trombone was often used as a chamber instrument; balance was not a problem, the baroque trombone being a more delicate and expressive instrument than its modern counterpart. Many of the Gabrieli works that we now think of as being for brass ensemble were originally for mixed consorts of solo strings or voices, lutes and brass. Long cadenzas for trombone are often found in works of the period. This one forms a bridge between sections and I have added a new ending so that it ends conclusively.

Hypochondria
JAN DISMAS ZELENKA (1679-1755)

Zelenka was a Bohemian bass player and composer who studied in Prague but worked mostly in Dresden. J.S. Bach knew and admired his work. This movement is taken from a manuscript which the composer entitled *Six Concertos Written in a Hurry in Prague*. It is most effective when played with a lively spring in its step and a lot should be made of the hairpins.

Dead March from Saul
GEORGE FRIDERICH HANDEL (1685-1759)

In baroque and classical times the sound of the trombone was strongly associated with death and the supernatural, and the original version of this march has the melody played by the trombone section, alternating with a pair of flutes. Handel wrote the tune a sixth higher, in C major, giving the high solo part to an alto trombone.

Anmerkungen

Che Faro Senza Eurydice?
Aus *Orpheus und Eurydike*
CHRISTOPH WILLIBALD VON GLUCK (1714-1787)

Orpheus singt die Arie "Ach, ich habe sie verloren", nachdem er seine Frau Eurydike, die er aus dem Totenreich in die Welt zurückführen darf, ein zweites Mal verliert: Er hat die Götter erzürnt, weil er sich umdrehte. Seine Klage wird unterbrochen durch den Gott Amor, der ihm Eurydike unter großem Jubel wiederschenkt. Es handelt sich um ein trauriges Stück, das aber nicht zu langsam gespielt werden sollte.

Polonaise Nr. 6
WILHELM FRIEDEMANN BACH (1710-1874)

Dieses eher nachdenkliche Stück ist ein gutes Beispiel des empfindsamen Stiles, der von Wilhelm Friedemann Bach und seinem Bruder Carl Philipp Emanuel gepflegt wurde. Man sollte das Tempo sehr flexibel behandeln und jede Phrase auskosten. In der originalen Tonart es-Moll klingt das Stück, wenn es auf einem nicht in gleichschwebender Temperatur gestimmten Instrument gespielt wird – zu Bachs Zeiten die Regel –, fast wie nicht von dieser Welt.

La Hieronyma
GIOVANNI MARTINO CESARE (c.1590-1667)

Cesare war ein in Bayern arbeitender Zinkspieler. Dieses Solostück ist einer Sammlung entnommen, die er 1621 publizierte. Allgemeine Kenntnisse der zeitgenössischen Aufführungspraxis waren damals so weit verbreitet, daß der Komponist nur wenige diesbezügliche Hinweise gab. Aus diesem Grund habe ich zahlreiche Angaben zur Dynamik und zur Phrasierung ergänzt, außerdem in der Klavierstimme die Möglichkeiten zur Imitation der Solostimme angegeben. Das Stück sollte wie improvisiert klingen.

Largo aus dem Cello-Konzert in Es-Dur
ANTONIO VIVALDI (1678-1741)

Der wegen seiner Haarfarbe als "Roter Priester" bekannte Vivaldi arbeitete in Venedig als Musikerzieher in einem für seine musikalischen Aufführungen berühmten Waisenhaus. Der Solopart sollte gesanglich gespielt werden; in diesem Tempo sind Achtelnoten relativ lange Noten. An den Stellen, wo die Intervalle größer werden, sollte man im Tempo lieber ein bißchen nachlassen, um die Tonqualität zu wahren.

Zwei Tänze: Volta und Pavan de Spaigne
MICHAEL PRAETORIUS (1571-1621)

Die *Volta* war ein lebhafter Paartanz. Bei jeder punktierten Note wurde die Dame von ihrem knienden Partner in die Luft geschleudert, wobei ihre Unterröcke und Knöchel sichtbar wurden. Dieses Stück darf also durchaus ein wenig frech klingen. Die *Pavan de Spaigne* war im Stil würdevoller, diese hier sollte sehr lyrisch interpretiert werden.

When I am Laid in Earth
Aus *Dido und Aeneas*
HENRY PURCELL (1659-1695)

Die Oper *Dido und Aeneas* wurde 1689 zur Aufführung an der Privatschule für junge Damen von Josiah Priest in Chelsea komponiert. Im dritten Akt singt die von ihrem Geliebten Aeneas zurückgewiesene Dido die berühmte Abschiedsarie "Werd' ich ins Grab gelegt." Die wiederholten Noten im zweiten Teil erklingen zu den Worten "Gedenke mein, ach, vergiss mein Los." Das Stück läßt sich auf der Posaune am besten wiedergeben, wenn es mit Schwung und dennoch bei intensiver Tonqualität gespielt wird.

Forlane
Aus *Les Sybarites*
JEAN PHILIPPE RAMEAU (1683-1764)

Rameau war Organist und Musiktheoretiker, der seinen besonderen Erfolg als Opernkomponist erst im Alter von 50 Jahren erreichte. Es handelt sich hier um einen ländlichen Tanz, der mit Schwung und unter deutlicher Betonung der Taktschwerpunkte musiziert werden sollte.

Allemande
Aus dem *4. Concert Royal*
FRANÇOIS COUPERIN (1668-1733)

Die *Concerts Royaux* wurden 1714-1715 zur sonntäglichen Unterhaltung Ludwig XIV in Versailles komponiert. Die Besetzung war nicht festgeschrieben; bei verschiedenen Anlässen wurden die Solopartien mit Violine, Oboe und Flöte besetzt. Die Musik wurde bei der Aufführung reich verziert. Die in unserer Ausgabe mitgeteilten Verzierungen liegen für die Posaune gut und dürften kein Problem bereiten, wenn sie gleichmäßig und mit einem guten Gefühl für die Linie ausgeführt werden.

Adagio und Allegro
Aus der *Sonate für 2 Violinen, Posaune und Continuo*
HEINRICH BIBER (1644-1704)

Im 17. Jahrhundert wurde die Posaune oft als kammermusikalisches Instrument benutzt. Die klangliche Balance war kein Problem, da die Posaune im Barock im Vergleich zur heutigen Posaune ein zarteres und ausdrucksvolleres Instrument war. Viele der Werke von Gabrieli, die wir heute als für Blechbläserensemble konzipiert halten, waren ursprünglich für gemischte Besetzungen mit Solostreichern oder Sängern, Lauten und Blechblasinstrumenten gedacht. In diesen Stücken gibt es häufig lange Kadenzen für die Posaune. Die hier mitgeteilte bildet die Verbindung zwischen zwei Abschnitten, wurde aber durch einen neuen Schluß ergänzt, so daß sie für sich stehen kann.

Hypochondria
JAN DISMAS ZELENKA (1679-1755)

Zelenka war ein böhmischer Kontrabassist und Komponist, der in Prag studierte, sein Leben aber vor allem in Dresden verbrachte. Johann Sebastian Bach kannte und schätzte sein Werk. Der Satz stammt aus einem vom Komponisten wie folgt betitelten Manuskript: "Sechs in Prag eilig geschriebene Konzerte". Am wirkungsvollsten ist das Stück wenn es lebhaft musiziert wird.

Totenmarsch aus Saul
GEORG FRIEDRICH HÄNDEL (1685-1759)

In Barock und Klassik wurde der Posaunenklang vielfach mit dem Tod oder auch mit Übernatürlichem assoziiert. In der originalen Fassung wird bei diesem Marsch die Melodie von der Posaunengruppe im Wechsel mit zwei Flöten musiziert. Händel schrieb den Marsch eine Sexte höher (C-Dur) und besetzte eine Altposaune in der höchsten Stimme.